Prayer Prevents Damage

A Spiritual Survival Kit

Bishop Archie McInnis, II

PRAYER PREVENTS DAMAGE
A Spiritual Survival Kit

Unless otherwise noted, all Scripture quotations are from the King James Version of the Bible.

Published by
Full Effect Gospel Ministries, Inc.
Brooklyn, NY

Edited by the Full Effect Editing Team
Wanza Leftwich, The Gospel Writer, www.wanzaleftwich.com
Cynthia McInnis, Author, Biblical Educator, Expositor

<u>Contact Us</u>:
Full Effect Gospel Ministries

900 New Lots Avenue   635 W Turner Street
Brooklyn, NY 11208   Allentown, PA 18102
718-927-0476   **610-351-2541**

DEDICATION

To my mom and dad
Bishop Archie L. McInnis, Sr. &
Elder Beverly McInnis

Thank you for waking me and my siblings up for 6am prayer every day as children. Your lifestyle of prayer has penetrated my life eternally. Thank you

TABLE OF CONTENTS

CHAPTER ONE
Prayer Is Necessary For Success

Because of the fall of man, prayer is quintessential to the survival of mankind. Sin separated us from God and consequently contaminated God's original intent for man. God put the original man, Adam, in the Garden of Eden where there was no lack, sickness or any spiritual imperfection in his life. There were no needs in Adam's life as long as he kept the word that God gave him in the garden.

God gave Adam clear instructions not to eat of the tree that was in the midst of the garden. As long as Adam obeyed God, he had a good and prosperous life in the garden. It was not until he chose to give in to the desire of his wife and ate the fruit of the tree that God forbade, that he suffered a consequence. This disobedience caused a separation between God and men. God said that if they ate from the tree that they would surely die; He was referring to a spiritual death, a state of separation from God. God is a spirit and they that worship him must worship him in spirit and in truth. (John 4:24) Man is also body, soul and spirit.

Now, man has lost his spiritual identity because of sin and can only identify with his body and soul, leaving him with a spiritual void. The body is the flesh that gives us world consciousness through the five senses; hearing, seeing, touching, tasting, and smelling. The soul is where the emotions are; the ability to reason (the mind). The spirit gives you God-consciousness. It is how we fellowship and communicate with God because God is a spirit. Sin brought spiritual death and cut off that connection between God, Adam and Eve. This makes prayer necessary.

Sin caused Adam and Eve to be more self-conscious. They pointed out that they saw themselves naked and covered themselves with leaves. But in creation God made them naked and they were naked and not ashamed. As long as they were connected to God spiritually, they were less self-conscious and more God-conscious. They saw themselves the way God saw them. Adam and Eve were pure in their thinking as long as they were spiritually alive.

Satan used the serpent which was more subtle than any other beast or animal that God had made. (Genesis 3:1) That serpent intrigued Eve through world consciousness; for, everything that is in the world is the lust of the flesh, the lust of the eyes and the pride of life (1 John 2:16). The serpent pointed out the tree that was in the midst of the garden and brought to Eve's attention that the tree was pleasant to look upon (the lust of the eyes) and that it was good for food (the lust of the flesh) and that it had the ability to make one wise (the pride of life). The serpent used world-consciousness to pull her away from God-consciousness. Once Adam and Eve bit the bait of Satan, through the serpent's deception, they became self-conscious and covered their nakedness with fig leaves. Isn't it amazing how in Mark 11 Jesus cursed a fig tree because it was covered with leaves but had no fruit? Sin brought on a curse of shame and unfruitfulness. Because of what they loss spiritually within, they had this need to cover up an outward nakedness (pride). They were, before, naked and not ashamed but the lust of the flesh, the lust of the eyes, the pride of life and other things choked the Word and they became unfruitful. Sadly, the devil has deceived some of us to cover ourselves with leaves while we produce no fruit! Leaves wither away but fruit has seed in it to keep producing life perpetually. (Mark 4)

Life is in the spirit and the devil knows that. That's why the devil works day and night trying to keep us carnally minded. Jesus said the words I speak to you are life and spirit. (John 6:63) As long as Adam and Eve held on to God's word they were spiritually alive. But sin brought spiritual death, (a separation from God). But Jesus Christ, through His obedience, gave us the right to be reconnected to God. (Romans 5:19)

Remember that the serpent was in the garden with Adam and Eve. God would be in the garden visiting too. When God came to the garden in the cool of the day looking for Adam and Eve they said that they hid themselves because they were naked.

God said, "Who told you that you were naked?" There were two voices that visited Adam and Eve in the garden; God and the serpent.   Who you communicate with the most has the most influence in your life. This is why prayer is necessary. Prayer is talking and hearing from God. The more we pray, the more we think like God.

If evil communications can corrupt good manners, (1 Corinthians 15:33) then it's best to avoid evil communication. Talk to God who communicates life and life more abundantly. Adam's failure to acknowledge God's word and his obedience to the voice of his wife to eat from the forbidden tree caused a catastrophic event in both of their lives. The voice you obey is critical to your destiny! Jesus said my sheep hear my voice and another they will not follow. (John 10:27) You learn God's voice in two ways: #1, you learn God's voice through His written word. God will not say anything contrary to his written word. When Jesus was tempted in the wilderness by the devil, he said to Jesus, if you be the son of God, turn this stone into bread; Jesus said, it is written, man shall not live by bread alone but by every word that proceeds out of the mouth of God. (Luke 4:3,4) Knowing the written word is critical to knowing the voice of God. #2, prayer helps us to hear the audible voice of God through our spirits.

In Acts, Chapter 10, God speaks to an Italian man by the name of Cornelius. Because of his prayers and giving, God spoke to him in a vision giving him instructions for a blessing. When you pray, God will talk back to you in your spirit through visions, dreams and an audible voice. God spoke to Abraham through visions and though his audible voice. Abraham prayed that God would not destroy Lot with Sodom and Gomorrah and the angel of the Lord spoke directly with Abraham as he made intercession for his nephew Lot. God speaks through messengers; people of God, angels, through visions, dreams and through his audible voice. God spoke to Moses on top of the mountain. These men of God prayed and they heard God's voice and they had great success.

God wants to bless us. God wants to deliver us. The Bible says, "If my people, which are called by my name, will humble themselves and pray and seek my face and turn from their wicked ways, then I will hear from heaven, forgive their sin and heal their land" (2 Chronicles 7:14). God gave man dominion over the earth in the book of Genesis and God is not an Indian giver. He wouldn't give us the earth and then take it back. God requires that we pray to invite him into our earthly situations so that he might bless us.

CHAPTER TWO
Prayer Is Spiritual With Physical Results

It is crucial to know that everything that is physical or natural exists because of the spiritual. Through faith we understand that the worlds were framed by the word of God, so that things which are seen were not made of things which do appear. (Hebrews 11:3)

We mentioned in the previous chapter that Jesus' words are spirit and life. Well, the word of faith has spiritual power to create physical things. The world, in Hebrews 11:3, is a physical world that is created by spiritual means or substance. There is an undercurrent to everything that we see with the natural eye. When you look at the ocean, for example, you can see waves or the current on the surface of the ocean but what is really causing the ocean to move, is coming from the bottom of the ocean not the top. Just because we can only see from the surface does not mean that what we see is the source of the movement. It is moving from the undercurrent which is unseen from the surface. Things that are seen are not made by things which do appear. (Hebrews 11:3) So, therefore, the things that we see have an undercurrent or spiritual force behind them.

When Adam and Eve ate from the forbidden tree, something spiritual happened in their minds, and they knew that they were naked and covered themselves with fig leaves because they were ashamed. Something as physical as a piece of fruit, caused them to change their minds, (which were unseen), and think differently about themselves. The undercurrent was that they received a lying word from the father of lies, Satan himself, and brought spiritual damnation upon themselves. There are unseen forces behind the words you speak and the words that you obey.   Satan's words bring spiritual death and destruction (John 10:10) but God's word gives spiritual life and healing. (Psalm 107:20)

If you only notice the surface of life, you will think that life is a matter of chance but when you look deeper you will begin to understand that life is a matter of choice (Deuteronomy 30:19). Words are spiritual. The earth continues to turn today because of the word of God that was spoken over it in the beginning of time. It is not happenstance or good fortune; it is the power of the word of God.

Words carry power (Proverbs 19:21).Words are unseen until written down on paper or manifested in deed. When words enter the ear of a person it causes them to think, then react. For instance, if I told you that your shoe laces were untied you would think about it and then look down to tie your shoe laces. My words to you were heard not seen but yet entered into your unseen mind and caused you to look down to tie a physical shoe lace. Simple but true. Words trigger the mind and cause a reaction. God used the foolishness of preaching to save those that believed (1Corinthians 1:21).

Motivational speaking and words of encouragement inspire men and women of all walks of life to accomplish incredible things. The right words can heal you and the wrong words can destroy you. We are where we are today because of the words that we chose to speak, believe, and live by (Mark 11:23).

Prayer is spiritual. When we pray, we pray to a God who is a spirit; a God that we have never seen before but we pray by faith, knowing that He hears us. The Bible says, ask and it shall be given...; (Luke 11:9) when we ask God for something, by faith, in prayer, the Word of God says that it shall be given. Prayer is between you and God. Prayer is a spiritual undertaking. It takes faith to pray. He that cometh to God must first believe that He is and that He is a rewarded of those who diligently seek him. (Hebrews 11:6) Praying in the spirit will get you results in the physical!

Hannah could not have children because she was barren but through prayer by faith she conceived and birthed a physical baby; something that she could touch and hold. Praying changed a physical condition in her body. She prayed to God, who is a spirit, but in return received physical results from her prayer.

The Scriptures speak of closet prayer; Jesus talks about that very clearly. He says that when you pray, go into your secret closet, the God that sees in secret shall reward you in the open. (Matthew 6:18) That sounds like physical results from a spiritual prayer to me. Secret prayer is when it's just you and God talking but God answers your prayer openly, meaning that your private prayer has obvious results in public. The key to this is faith. You have to have confidence in God when you pray. Know that God cannot lie. God is holy. Holy means devoted and dedicated. God is devoted and dedicated to His word to perform it in your life.

If God's word can create heaven and earth and maintain it until now, He can keep every promise in His word that He has promised to those that believe. Have faith in God.

CHAPTER THREE
Prayer Is a Weapon

"Praying always with all prayer and supplication in the Spirit, and watching thereunto with all perseverance and supplication for all saints;" (Ephesians 6:18)

From the creation of man, the devil has declared war on mankind. John 10:10 says that the thief (devil) comes to kill, steal and destroy. We must know that there is a spiritual warfare going on and like it or not we are in it. The devil is the prince of the power of the air, meaning that he has power in certain regions and other places in the earth that are not normally recognized with the natural eye.

"Wherein in time past ye walked according to the course of this world, according to the prince of the power of the air, the spirit that now worketh in the children of disobedience:" (Ephesians 2:2)

Satan is the unseen god who lies underneath, guiding the course of this world, blinding the minds of unbelievers. (2 Cor. 4:4) Because Satan is a spirit, he is able to get the advantage on carnal minded people. "For we wrestle not against flesh and blood but against principalities, against powers, against the rulers of the darkness of this world, against spiritual wickedness in high places." (Ephesians 6:12)

The battle that we are facing is a spiritual battle. For, though we walk in the flesh, we do not war after the flesh. (2 Corinthians 10:3) (For the weapons of our warfare are not carnal, but mighty through God to the pulling down of strong holds). (2 Corinthians 10:4) This is a spiritual fight and God would not have us to be ignorant concerning the devil's devices. In order to defeat the devil at his game, we must be spiritually minded. The spiritual mind can identify the enemy and defeat him through the power of God. "Let this mind be in you, which was also in Christ Jesus." (Philippians 2:5)

Christ defeated the devil and we can do the same thing through Christ Jesus. No weapon that is formed against us shall prosper... (Isaiah 54:17) because we walk in the spirit, not after the flesh. (Romans 8:1,4) Walking in the spirit is obeying the word of God. Jesus said the words I speak are spirit and life. (John 6:63) So when we obey God's word we walk in spiritual authority; when we disobey God's word, we are under Satan's influence.

According to Ephesians 2:2, if we walk according to the course of this world, we are operating in the spirit of disobedience. Why? I'm glad you asked, because this world's system is governed by the prince of the power of the air.... Then the rest of that verse goes on to say this, "the spirit that now worketh in the children of disobedience..." See, the devil is a spirit and when we walk in disobedience to God's word we are operating under satanic influence; that's spiritual warfare.

Whether you express obedience to God or assimilation to the world's system, which is governed by Satan, will determine whose side you are on in this battle! The word of God says, "Be not conformed to this world but be ye transformed by the renewing of your mind." (Romans 12:2) Remember, 2 Corinthians 4:4 says that the god of this world has blinded the minds of the unbelievers. The mind is the battleground where the warfare festers. This is why the Bible says gird up the loins of your mind (1 Peter 1:13) Loins represent below-the-belt, vulnerabilities or weak areas where the devil may attack you.

Ephesians 6:14 says, "stand therefore, having your loins girt about with truth...." "Stand", is a war term. Stand for what you believe, take a stand for righteousness etc. Stand having your loins girt about with truth. It is the truth that makes us free from the bondage of Satan. Jesus said, "And ye shall know the truth and the truth will make you free." (John 8:32) In order to win in spiritual warfare you have to know the truth. Jesus said, "If you continue in my word then are you my disciples."(John 8:31) A disciple is a student. We must be students of the word of God so that we may know the truth and that truth makes us free.

Truth is not a statement. Truth is a person. Jesus said, "I am the WAY, the TRUTH and the LIFE.... (John 14:6) That is why whatever we do in word or in deed should be done in the name of Jesus. (Colossians 3:17) There is power in the name of Jesus. When contending with the devil, use the word of God which has authority over the devil. Even Michael, the Archangel, defeated Satan by saying, "The Lord God rebuke thee" (Jude 1:9). The devil cannot stand against the word of God. Every chain will break in Jesus' name.

You might not know the whole Bible but if you know Jesus, you have the totality of the word of God in His name and the devil cannot defeat you. In the beginning was the Word and the Word was with God and the Word was God" (John 1:1) "and the Word was made flesh..." (John 1:14) Jesus is the living word of God. Use the name of Jesus and win. If we have the mind of Christ, which is the word of God, in us, when we pray to the Father, in Jesus name, He answers our prayer. Jesus said, "If ye abide in me, and my words abide in you, ye shall ask what ye will, and it shall be done unto you." (John 15:7)

When we recognize that Jesus is the "Way, the Truth and the Life," our lives become wrapped up in His will. His will becomes our will and when we ask what we will, which is His will, then His will shall be done. See, Jesus' will was so much God's will, that when Jesus prayed, He said, "Not my will but thy will be done" (Luke 22:42). God will answer your prayer when your will is lined up with His will.

The disciples asked Jesus, "Lord teach us to pray..." "And he said unto them, when ye pray, say, Our Father which art in heaven, Hallowed be thy name. Thy kingdom come. Thy will be done, as in heaven, so in earth." (Luke 11:1,2). When we are properly connected to God, we pray His will. God's will is that none should perish. (2 Peter 3:9) Jesus came that we might have life more abundantly. (John 10:10) God's will is that we prosper and be in health even as our soul prospers. (3 John 1:2)

When we know God's will, prayer becomes a joy and not a burden. Daniel was a praying man and favor was all over his life even in a strange land. Prayer invokes the presence of God and causes the Father's will for us in heaven to be done for us on earth. In heaven, God has dominion. God gave mankind dominion on the earth but in the Garden of Eden, Satan took that dominion by deception; but when we are in a right relationship with God, we reclaim dominion through prayer. "If my people, which are called by my name, shall humble themselves, and pray, and seek my face, and turn from their wicked ways; then will I hear from heaven, and will forgive their sin, and will heal their land." (2 Chronicles 7:14). Prayer is our weapon of warfare. We cannot win without it.

CHAPTER FOUR
The Prayer Bill

"And he spake a parable unto them to this end, that men ought always to pray, and not to faint;" (Luke 18:1) Prayer is not an option. Jesus said pray that you enter not into temptation for the spirit is willing but the flesh is weak. (Matthew 26:41) It is not the spirit that isn't willing to pray but it is the flesh or the carnal mind. The spirit indeed longs for its God. Because His spirit bears witness with our spirit that we are the children of God. (Romans 8:16) Without the presence of God, our spirit is void and barren but with His spirit we are powerful and full of life. Like a fish without water is dead so is our spirit without God.

Prayer is spiritual because we communicate with God who is a spirit. Man is body, soul and spirit, so if we don't feed our spirit our spirit becomes spiritually dead and, ultimately, we live a life based on carnality instead of spirituality. Prayer keeps us spiritually connected to heaven. Prayer opens the heaven unto us. Jacob prayed until angels began to descend and ascend from heaven. It was so real that Jacob was able to wrestle with an angel.

There are so many possibilities when we pray. But the lack of prayer can lead to failure and disappointment. In the Garden of Gethsemane, Jesus told Peter to pray with Him but Peter and the other disciples with him fell asleep during prayer. Because they forfeited that opportunity and gave in to sleep, they missed seeing Jesus move from low strength to more strength. "And there appeared an angel unto him from heaven, strengthening him". (Luke 22:43)

It does not matter what the issue is, God will strengthen you if you pray. Jesus was down and was tempted to forfeit going to the cross but He prayed and an angel came down from heaven to strengthen Him. Prayer gives us access to Heaven's resources.

The devil is constantly on the prowl seeking whom he may devour. (1 Peter 5:8) So, prayer is a must. There is an enemy loose and his name is Satan. Jesus told Peter that Satan desires to have you and sift you as wheat but Jesus said but I have prayed for you. (Luke 22:31) Satan will not let up until the Day of Judgment. So, praying always is an absolute requirement to maintain strength in the battle. Prayer wears down the enemy.

In Luke 18, Jesus gives us a parable about a woman who is a widow. The word, "widow" implies here that she is desolate, weak and defenseless. She goes to an unjust judge who does not fear God expecting to get justice. She has an enemy in this text that appears as an oppressor or as oppression. The unjust judge avenges her, which means he redeems her from the oppression, because of her continual coming. She didn't stop coming to that judge for the same reason day and night. The judge in the parable was annoyed by the widow. So he granted her the request that she petitioned him for. This is saying that prayer should be continual until you get what you've been praying for. "And he spake a parable unto them to this end, that men ought to always pray, and not to faint." (Luke 18:1)

The widow troubled the judge until she wore him down. In prayer, sometimes you have to knock until the door is opened. "Ask and it shall be given, seek and ye shall find, knock and the door shall be opened."(Matthew 7:7) A knocking prayer is repetitive. If you know that what you need is on the other side of a door and you know that someone is on the other side of that door and has the ability to open the door and let you in, you are going to continue knocking.

Sometimes there is warfare going on in the spirit realm that is holding up your request. Just like what happened to Daniel. But Daniel kept on praying until Michael, the warring angel got the advantage in a spiritual battle with the Prince of Persia, which is a fallen angel that manipulated the King of Persia. However, Michael, the archangel, prevailed against him and Gabriel, the messaging angel, was now able to get God's answer to Daniel. Gabriel told him that God heard him the first time when he prayed but the prince of Persia withstood him for 21 days. (Daniel 10:13) Just like God answered Daniel's prayer, God will answer your prayers. Don't faint because you didn't get an answer right away. Pray knowing that God heard you the first time you prayed. You may say, "If God heard me the first time, why keep on praying?" Like Daniel, pray until you get your answer. Like the widow woman in the parable, don't quit until you are avenged of your oppressor or the oppression!

Remember, when you pray, there is warfare in the spirit world trying to hinder your answer. But God has all power and can never be defeated. Pray in every season for every reason. Pray because you love talking to God. Pray because you love hearing from God. Pray with all prayer and supplication. Supplications are special prayers of blessings; prayers averting evils which we fear.

There is so much to pray for; family, healing, friends, finances, our world leaders etc. Somebody needs your prayers. The Bible says pray one for another. (James 5:16) Pray for them that despitefully use you.(Luke 6:28)

Pray for the saints. Pray for your church. Have you approached every issue with prayer?

Jesus said, mankind should always pray. There are bills that can be eliminated like a car note, house mortgage, college tuition, etc. But there are some bills that are reoccurring bills, like electric, insurance, groceries, and day to day necessities that cannot be avoided. Just like you meet those bills, please don't forget the Prayer Bill. You owe it to God and to yourself. Your Prayer Bill is past due! Always pray.

CHAPTER FIVE
Prayer Prevents Damage

"Now when Daniel knew that the writing was signed, he went into his house; and his windows being open in his chamber toward Jerusalem, he kneeled upon his knees three times a day, and prayed, and gave thanks before his God, as he did aforetime." (Daniel 6:10)

Daniel was used to taking a stand for God. As a child, captive in Babylon, he purposed in his heart not to defile himself with Babylonian customs. The king appointed a daily provision of meat and wine from his table, to feed Daniel for nourishment. But the King's food and drink were also offered to Pagan gods. It was the custom to throw a small part of the meat and wine upon the ground, as a sacred offering to the gods, so as to consecrate their feast.

To have taken part in such an act would have been to sanction idolatry. But God gave Daniel favor with king Nebuchadnezzar's chief official, Ashpenaz. When you decide to stand for God, God will stand for you. God had brought Daniel into favor and tender love with Ashpenaz, meaning that God had established faithful loyalty between Daniel and Ashpenaz. There is no evidence of Daniel being rude, making a scene or being disrespectful in his determination not to defile himself. Water puts out fires and a soft answer turns away wrath.(Proverbs 15:1) Sometimes even though we are right in principle, we can be wrong in behavior which can cause oppositions instead of accommodations. Daniel made a request to Ashpenaz, the chief official under king Nebuchadnezzar, not to eat the King's food that he might not defile himself and with tough negotiations, Daniel's request was granted.

Daniel requested water and vegetables. This afforded Daniel to be nourished without defiling himself. Certain indulging affects divine sensitivity. Consecration and sanctification keeps your spirit open to revelation. "No man that warreth entangleth himself with the affairs of this life; that he may please him who hath chosen him to be a soldier." (2 Timothy 2:4). "Be sober, be vigilant; because your adversary the devil, as a roaring lion, walketh about, seeking whom he may devour:" (1 Peter 5:8). But just as He who called you is holy, so be holy in all you do; (1 Peter 1:15 NIV).

Holy means devoted and dedicated. Dedication of a soldier is required to fight in any war, spiritually or physically. Daniel's purpose caused his three friends to have purpose. Hananiah, Mishael and Azariah stood with Daniel. Your purpose will cause others to get purpose!

Even if their purpose is just to stand with you in your purpose.

Daniel and his three friends ate less but looked better. Ashpenaz's job was to find good-looking young men without defects, skilled in all wisdom, possessing knowledge, conversant with learning, and capable of serving in the king's palace. Ashpenaz had three years to train them to work in the King's palace. These children were both picked out of the Israelites and the Babylonians. When it was time to be presented to the king, Daniel and his friends, that ate less were ten times better than the rest. When you work your purpose, less becomes more.

Daniel and his friends appeared before the king better, fairer and fatter. When you purpose in your heart to be faithful, you will have a B.F.F; you will be Better, Fairer and Fatter. Fatter, meaning, Good; (Isaiah 55:2) having the Fat of the land. Glory!!!

See, Ashpenaz risked his life by not letting Daniel and his friends eat the portion of the King's meat and by not letting them drink the king's wine. Ashpenaz could have been killed for disobeying the King's order but because of Daniel's purpose and faithfulness to God, those that took the risk and stood with him had no damage.

In the book of Daniel, Chapter 2, verse 1, it is recorded that King Nebuchadnezzar started to dream dreams. His dreams troubled his spirit so that he could not sleep. One day the king called for the wise men of Babylon so that they could interpret his dreams. So, naturally, the wise men, who were astrologers, magicians and sorcerers, asked the king to tell them what he had dreamed so they could give him the interpretation, but the king made an outrageous request to the wise men to tell *him* what he had dreamed *and* to interpret the dream! That was a request that was unheard of to them.

The king was adamant about it. He said that he could not remember his dream so he wanted his gifted wise men to reveal to him what he had dreamed and interpret it. The wise men of Babylon told him that there was not a man who could do such a thing as to know his dream without him telling it and expect him to interpret it too. It's one thing to interpret the dream but how can you interpret a dream that is unknown? In other words, the wise men told the king that his request was impossible.

So the king was very angry and commanded to destroy all the wise men of Babylon. Now there was a panic in Babylon amongst the wise men. The wise men of Babylon were about to be executed. But Daniel heard the commotion and was told about the king's decree that all the wise men of Babylon were to be killed including Daniel and his three friends. Daniel went and made this thing known to his three friends, Hananiah, Mishael, and Azariah and they united in prayer! They made intercession.

The Hebrew word for intercession is the word PAGA. Vine's dictionary and Strong's dictionary have a two-fold meaning for intercession that almost seems contradictory, however, it shows the two main aspects of the word:

<u>Vine's Dictionary</u>
. To collide with
. To encroach
. To drive in
. To strike up against
. To be violent against

<u>Strong's Dictionary</u>
. To invade
. To come in between
. To entreat
. To meet together
. Intercession or to pray
. To be a peace-maker

The power of intercession is amazing. These guys prayed until God revealed the king's secret dream to Daniel in a night vision (Daniel 2:19). My God! There was terror going through Babylon that night because of the king's decree but there was a prayer meeting going on at night that caused God to reveal a secret!

You could be having a night season in your life right now but if you pray, God will give you night vision. One vision in the middle of the night can turn your night into day, your sorrow into gladness, your pain into praise.

"Then Daniel blessed the God of Heaven". Daniel had not even given the revelation of the dream to the king yet but he praised God once he knew the secret was revealed to him. Praise God for the idea, the strategy, or the revelation before you even act on it. God's word shall not return unto Him void. (Isaiah 55:11) So, you do not have to wait to see the manifestation. Once you get a word from God, it's already done. Praise Him now!

Daniel told King Nebuchadnezzar his dream and interpreted it. No man had ever done that before. According to the wise men of Babylon, it was impossible to be done but God is amazing. Daniel and his friends entreated God through prayer and accomplished the supernatural. What's impossible with man is possible with God.

Gifts, rewards and great honor was promised to the one who could tell the dream and interpret it. King Nebuchadnezzar fell prostrate before Daniel and paid him honor and ordered that an offering and incense be presented to him. The king said to Daniel, "Surely your God is the God of gods and the Lord of kings and a revealer of mysteries, for you were able to reveal this mystery." Then the king placed Daniel in a high position and lavished many gifts on him. He made him ruler over the entire province of Babylon and placed him in charge of all its wise men. (Daniel 2:46-48 NIV) Moreover, at Daniel's request the king appointed Shadrach, Meshach and Abednego administrators over the province of Babylon, while Daniel himself remained at the royal court. (Daniel 2:49 NIV).

God blessed Daniel with honor and lavish gifts. Daniel was also promoted in Babylon. He was made ruler over of the province of Babylon. Not only that but because of Daniel and his friends praying, their prayers prevented harm from coming to them and to the wise men of Babylon. Prayer can cover the just and the unjust. Just because of you and your connection to God, those who are in the same boat with you will not perish. Ask the Apostle Paul. No doubt, he was a praying man. He would tell you that on his way to Rome, as a prisoner, they experienced a great storm called Euroclydon (Acts 27:14) but no man's life was lost (Acts 27:22). The ship did not make it but every soul did.

You may have lost some things in your life but you didn't lose your life and your soul and your spirit has no damage. *Prayer Prevents Damage.*

Now, King Nebuchadnezzar made an image of gold and set it up for everyone to worship it. It seems crazy, after experiencing God through Daniel with the revelation and interpretation of his dream, King Nebuchadnezzar still worshipped Pagan gods. It's amazing how you can see the supernatural power of God and still not change your ways. King Nebuchadnezzar commanded that everyone would bow down to worship the golden image when they heard the music playing. Daniel's friends refused to worship the image.

The same men that prayed to God with Daniel for the revelation and interpretation of the King's dream were now faced with more opposition because of their commitment to Jehovah God. They were questioned by the king and threatened to be thrown into the fiery furnace because of their refusal to bow. They could have bowed and not worshipped with their hearts to save their lives, some would say, but they were bold. They had confidence in their God and knew that if they bowed with their heads they were saying yes to idolatry and denying the true God like Peter denied Christ.

Fear and intimidation are detrimental to your destiny. I believe Peter loved Jesus and it's proven that he did but his fear got the best of him at the time of our Lord's trial and crucifixion. To deny Him is to be ashamed of Him. Do not ever be ashamed of the God we serve just to save your own pride. Stand up for Jesus Christ and do not bow down to the antics of this world.

Jesus said, "He that saves his life shall lose it but he that loses his life for Christ's sake shall save it." (Matthew 16:25) That is exactly what happened to Daniel's three friends. They were willing to lose their lives for God and saved it instead. This is what they told the king: "If our God—the one we serve—is able to rescue us from the furnace of flaming fire and from your power, Your Majesty, then let him rescue us. But if he doesn't, know this for certain, Your Majesty: we will never serve your gods or worship the gold statue you've set up." (Daniel 3:17-18 CEB)

Wow! What courage for God! They loved God with their lives. They were willing to give up their own lives for God. Love casteth out all fear. (1 John 4:18) True love is when you can worship God with your whole life. "Greater love hath no man than this, that a man lay down his life for his friends" (John 15:13) Jesus said, "Henceforth I call you not servants; for the servant knoweth not what his lord doeth: but I have called you friends; for all things that I have heard of my Father I have made known unto you." (John 15:15)

It seems like when you are about to lose everything, God gives you more than expected. When you take a stand for God, God is going to stand for you. The king was so furious by their declaration that he ordered the fire in the furnace to be turned up seven times more than it was normally heated. Some of you are under an unusual attack right now because regardless to your circumstances you have declared that you are standing on the promises of God.

The fire will not hurt you. The king commanded the mightiest men that were in his army to bind Shadrach, Meshach and Abednego which were the new names the king gave Daniel's friends. See, you have to watch who names you. Whoever names you, claims you. The king did not realize that these men belonged to the God who created the heavens and earth.

When they casted them into the fire, the king was astounded at the fact that the fire, so heated, slew the mighty men that threw Shadrach, Meshach and Abednego into the fire. He jumped up in haste to see what would befall these men in the fire and saw four men instead of three. He said to his associates, "Did not we throw three men in the fire?" They responded, "Certainly king." The king said, "Look, I see four men loose, walking in the midst of the fire, and they have no hurt; and the form of the fourth is like the son of God."

These men were thrown in the fire bound but ended up loose with no hurt to them, walking in the middle of the fire. Wow. The son of God was in the fire with them. Now, nobody saw The Lord get into the fire but one thing is for sure, He was in there! You might not see God but know that God is with you. The only one that we know of in this story, who saw the son of God in the fire was King Nebuchadnezzar; I heard Rev. Samuel Rodriguez say that, "There is no evidence that even Shadrach, Meshach, and Abednego saw the son of God in the fire. But we know that Jesus, the son of God was in the fire because the enemy saw Him."

Sometimes you do not see God in your situation but the devil does. The king called for them to come out of the fire and the king's associates witnessed these men come out of a fire that had no power upon them. We know that the fire was powerful because it slew the King's men. But that same fire had no power on the men that were men of the King of Kings and The Lord of Lords. Jesus Christ is Lord of all.

Shadrach, Meshach and Abednego changed the king's words, meaning that the king's law and decree to worship the golden image was changed. On top of that, King Nebuchadnezzar promoted Shadrach, Meshach and Abednego in the province of Babylon. This boldness that these men of God had could not be so if it were not for their love for God and a life of prayer.

Daniel prayed three times a day no matter what.

When Daniel learned that a document had been signed forbidding anyone to pray to another God, he went to his house. Now, his upper room had open windows that faced Jerusalem. Daniel knelt down, prayed, and praised his God three times that day, just like he always did. (Daniel 6:10 CEB)

There was not anything that could stop Daniel from keeping his time of prayer with God. He prayed continually. Prayer protects you. "At evening, morning, and midday I complain and moan so that God will hear my voice. He saves me, unharmed, from my struggle, though there are many who are out to get me. God, who is enthroned from ancient days, will hear and humble them. Selah. Because they don't change and they don't worship God." (Psalms 55:17-19 CEB)

Daniel understood where his help came from. Even with much success in a country where he rose from slavery into one of the top men in Babylon. He did not take it for granted that God was his source of help. Promotion comes from The Lord.

Daniel had an excellent spirit and I know that excellent spirit was birthed out of his prayer life and his love for God. Daniel dealt with some people who were jealous of his success. They tricked the new king, King Darius, into signing a decree that permitted anyone from praying to any other God for 30 days. This law was setup to trap Daniel because they could not find any fault with is work or character.

King Darius desired to make Daniel head of his operation because Daniel was that trustworthy. His co-workers were angry and wanted to stop Daniel's progress. The gates of hell shall not prevail. Hell wants to use its gates to stop your borders from expanding. The devil doesn't mind where you are, he just doesn't want you to go any further. So Daniel's co-workers or the king's administrative staff used his faith against him. The devil loves to use what God blessed you with, against you.

I've seen people join a church and love it. God blessed them there, they began to grow then all of a sudden they started to complain about the blessing God gave them. You have to remember that once there is promotion in your future all hell will come after you to stop it.

The decree was signed and it could not be changed by the Medo-Persian law. The punishment for praying to another God was to be thrown into the lion's den. But Daniel kept on praying. They found Daniel praying as he had always done. Daniel was arrested and could not be saved by king Darius because the punishment was death; to be eaten by lions. Darius, the king, favored Daniel and said, 'Your God shall deliver you." Death and life is in the power of the tongue. (Proverbs 18:21)

Whether the king realized it or not, he spoke powerful words of life. The Bible says the king could not eat or sleep while Daniel was in the lion's den but early in the morning the king called for Daniel and Daniel spoke from the lion's den saying, "O king live forever. God has sent His angel and shut the lion's mouths." Daniel came out of the lion's den with no damage. God sent His angel and shut the lion's mouths. If you pray, God will shut up the mouths of your enemies that are trying to assassinate your character. Prayer and a life of prayer prevent damage. The king ordered the ones that accused Daniel to be thrown into the lion's den and the lions killed them. What could not kill Daniel got rid of his enemies. Pray and God will fight your battles. Prayer Prevents Damage.

Other Ministry products available at
www.effect900.com

Get Your Copy Today!

**GOD NEVER LEAVES YOU
EMPTY HANDED;
YOU ALREADY HAVE WHAT
IT TAKES TO INCREASE!**

B.A.L.M.2
Bishop Archie L. McInnis, II

Follow the Bishop
Facebook.com/PrayerPreventsDamage
Twitter@ArchieMcInnisII
Instagram@ArchieMcInnisII